John Scott

A Letter to the Right Honourable Edmund Burke

Paymaster General of His Majesty's Forces

John Scott

A Letter to the Right Honourable Edmund Burke
Paymaster General of His Majesty's Forces

ISBN/EAN: 9783744763936

Printed in Europe, USA, Canada, Australia, Japan

Cover: Foto ©ninafisch / pixelio.de

More available books at **www.hansebooks.com**

A LETTER

TO THE

RIGHT HONOURABLE

EDMUND BURKE,

PAYMASTER GENERAL

OF HIS

MAJESTY's FORCES.

BY

MAJOR JOHN SCOTT.

LONDON:

PRINTED FOR J. STOCKDALE, OPPOSITE
BURLINGTON HOUSE, PICCADILLY.

M.DCC.LXXXIII.

A

LETTER

TO THE

RIGHT HONOURABLE

EDMUND BURKE.

Right Honourable Sir,

IN the diftribution of different parts to the minifterial orators who fupport the new India bill, in the
application of their different powers to this one important objeft, it was natural that all the topics
which afforded play to a wandering imagination, and
to tragic defcription, fhould have been allotted to
Mr. Burke. The field of fancy is almoft exclu-
fively your's; and when it was refolved, that in or-

der

der to palliate the intended invasion of our charter
and our property, the atrocious acts of barbarity
and cruelty committed by the servants of the East-
India Company abroad, should be held up to the
detestation of the House, and of the public, and
form one grand engine of the attack, your talents
both for the *pathetic* and the *fabulous*, gave you a
double claim to this branch of the service. Your
feelings are so tremblingly acute, your nerves are
so strung to compassion, your language is so attuned
to lamentation, that forms of horror and distress,
scenes of destruction and desolation, seem to arise
spontaneously in your mind, and to occupy that portion of the sensorium, which, in men of irritable
habits, is the province of reason, of judgment, and of
common sense. I am, therefore, one of those who
were exceedingly surprised that the right honourable
framer of the new bill should so palpably have en-
croached upon your privilege in his late harangues,
as to exhibit a very glowing and highly-coloured pic-
ture of the inhumanities of our countrymen in India. There is honour among thieves: surely it
cannot be wanting among Ministers. But I shall
hereafter be less inclined to wonder at any unwarrantable attempt to invade the prerogatives of the
subject,

subject, since I have seen, among yourselves, so
glaring an invasion of your's!

If avarice and rapacity were subjects open to the
eloquence of Mr. Fox, the tortures, the bloodshed
that accompanied them were themes that appertained
solely to Mr. Burke. The right honourable *Secretary* might inveigh as he pleased on the manner in
which the debts due to the Company had been con-
tracted—but it belonged to the right honourable
Paymaster to expatiate on the severities necessary for
extorting payment of them. In short, Sir, you
have been superseded in your functions : *The* Minis-
ter, who is soon to unite in his own person the rights
of the Company, the powers of the Crown, and
the riches of the East, has begun his career of injustice by excluding you from the path in which you
hoped to have trodden without a rival. *He* snatched
from your hands Colonel Boujour's letter—*He* told
the piteous tale of Cheyt Sing, the woes of Asophrul
Dowla, and the misfortunes of his grandmother !
I wonder you can ever forgive him. To take your
long prepared victim out of your clutches, to go out
of his way, and against his own repeated professions,
for the sake of abusing the Governor General of

Bengal,

Bengal, and to abuse him too for a sanguinary, murderous disposition, of which till that moment you had prided yourself (and with reason) as the sole discoverer, was a hard trial of your patience. But to drive you from every strong hold of your Committee, to leave you nothing but the stale defence of Shah Allum, the expulsion of that virtuous monarch Coffim Ally, and the defraudation of that disinterested Plenipotentiary, Omichund, whereon to erect your plea of participation in the spoils of Hindostan, must engage your very opponents in your behalf. They cannot but have beholden with an eye of pity the shifts to which you were driven, the distress in which you were involved by the necessity of a vague and uninteresting retrospection.

To plunge into the forgotten abyss of distant revolutions, to revive the convicted slander of artificial famines, to tread on the tender ground of injurious monopolies previous to the year 1772, *(with your friend General Smith at your elbow)* was indeed a bitter pill — but gilded as it is with five and twenty thousand a year from Government to yourself and your relations, you contrived somehow or other to swallow it: and even now that it is down, it cannot

fail,

fail, I think, to excite a few qualms — for you muft, at times be apprehenfive that your language and your conduct on former ftruggles with refpect to India, fhould live in the world's recollection: that it fhould be whifpered how ftrenuous and how loud an advocate you were in the year 1772 for the chartered rights of the Eaft-India Company. How you then reprobated the minifterial iniquity of your now-noble friend Lord North — How warmly you defended the innocence of the Company's fervants of *that* day — and how quickly, upon a proper application, *pulveris exigui jactu*, you can " renounce your princi-" ples, and eat your words."

In this formal recantation of your un-penfioned habits of thinking and fpeaking, Mr. Woodfall has been particularly cautious not to omit that you were up your legs upwards of two hours. This is a morfel information for us out of doors only. The membe who retired to dinner when you got up, knew the had full two hours of fpare time; and when returned, you had not fat down. But as you only fomewhat more than two hours to dif you had taken in during three years of har and as in that time you contrived to unfay e

that you had been heard to utter on the difcuffion of
the Regulating Act of the 13th of the King, I muft
allow that you performed it *with great expedition*,
with an expedition proportioned to the *neceffities of
the times*, and to the hurry of the whole tranfaction.
The fpeech which Mr. Woodfall has made for you in
Tuefday's Chronicle, deals fo exceedingly in *generals*,
that I cannot follow up with that accuracy and clofe-
nefs which I am inclined to beftow upon the fubject
your "prodigious detail of the conduct of the Company in Afia, from their firft eftablifhment there."
But I muft be permitted to remark, that it is fomewhat extraordinary to obferve you oftentatioufly
vaunting your late three-years courfe of ftudy, as the
ground of your claim to the attention of the Houfe,
when it is notorious to the moft fuperficial obferver
of your Reports, that every object of enquiry in your
committee, has been religioufly confined to the fingle
period of Mr. Haftings's adminiftration, and when
it is evident, from the whole tenour of your oration,
that you had been almoft expreffly referred, by a minifterial mandate, to events antecedent to that adminiftration. One article was indeed generoufly given
up to you, wherein there was a poffibility of implicat-
ing the Governor General :—a hiftory of that pomp-

ous

ous non-entity, *the mildeſt of Monarchs*, that Allum.
His *mildneſs* however I ſhall leave in your quiet poſ-
feſſion; for that quality has been ſeldom diſputed to
Monarchs who were without ſubjects. But that
he is " the moſt beneficent, humane," (i. e. *mild*
once more) " generous," (i. e. *beneficent*) " wiſe,
philoſophical," (*wiſe* again) " and religious of men,"
I muſt a little conteſt with you, notwithſtanding
your ingenious reduplication of epithets. Of his
beneficence I cannot at once recollect an inſtance,
except a donation (hardly gratuitous) of two lacs of
rupees—and that portion of his merits you ſhould
have left to the panegyric of General Smith. In
wiſdom I hold him greatly inferior to the Raja of
Tanjore; for in the *choice of friends*, which is one
great criterion of judgement, the latter has infinitely
the advantage. His religion, as it is that of a Ma-
hometan, is of little conſideration in a Chriſtian
aſſembly; and you had better have given him a good
ſhare of morality; however, I muſt acknowledge
to have heard, that his Majeſty is famous for copy-
ing the Koran with peculiar neatneſs of character,
and that he is not much interrupted in this auguſt
employment by attention to the management of his
extenſive empire, and to the welfare of his innume-
rable

rable fubjects. Between ourfelves, Sir——He is a
weak man. Lord Clive gave him the provinces of
Corah and Illahabad, which would afford him a
handfome maintenance, and were five times as much
as he could ever have acquired in any part of India
without us : and we alfo allowed him twenty-fix lacs
of rupees yearly from Bengal for the fupport of his
dignity. But he was too much of a *philofopher* to
attach himfelf to the good things of this world, fo
threw himfelf into the arms of his natural, here-
ditary, and conftitutional enemies the Marattas; ceded
to them, *without our confent,* the provinces we had
given him, and undertook a chimerical expedition to
Dehli. Are you furprifed that we took thofe provinces back again, when the King could not, or would
not, keep them ? or that we did not continue him
the fubfidy of twenty-fix lacs of rupees to be lavifhed
away among Marattas? Self-prefervation forced
upon us the conduct we obferved on that occafion ;
it was warmly approved *at home,* by both ends of
the town ; and it certainly has contributed more than
any other caufe, to keep Bengal ftill in our hands.
I hope the new Commiffioners will now afford this
great and virtuous Prince fome folid inftance of their
compaffion — and that they will reftore him thofe

provinces,

provinces, or some others in their stead, as well as his subsidy—by way of contrast to the measures of Mr. Hastings.—In the " Magna Charta of Hindof-" tan," it would be a miserable oversight to omit the Great Mogul ; and surely he has a claim upon the justice of the state, and still more upon the gratitude of individuals, for restitution of his countries and revenues.

It does not indeed perfectly meet my comprehension how you could explain the circumstance of the *sale* of this monarch to Sujah Dowla, nor the *sale* of Sujah Dowla *to himself*. No doubt you made this matter perfectly clear to your scanty remnant of an audience, but Mr. Woodfall has sunk the particulars. I know very well, that when his beneficent and philosophical Majesty ran away, we re-assumed the provinces which he chose to evacuate. I know that as they were too difficult to be managed by us, we parted with them for a valuable consideration to Sujah Dowla; by which means we strengthened our own frontier against the Marattas. I know also, that upon various occasions on which we afforded powerful military assistance, or important political services to Sujah Dowla, we endeavoured to balance the ac-

C   count

count in some degree, by stipulations for a pecuniary
return. If, however, that Visier purchased *himself*
by any of those transactions, he certainly thought
himself a gainer by the bargain : and as there is evidence before the Select Committee, that he lived and
died *in perfect indepenence,* it is manifest that, in this
instance at least, the Company broke through the
system of treachery, dishonesty, and injustice, with
which you have charged them, by leaving Sujah
Dowla in full and quiet possession of himself, after
they had thus sold him to himself.

So you have asserted that " that they sold Ragoba to
" the Marattas, and the Marattas to Ragoba." What
a childish play upon words! Did we not in the same
manner sell America to France and France to America ? What is there in the resolutions respecting Ragoba to justify such indecent puerilities ? Our Bombay Council had seen *that* Chief the ostensible and
the avowed head of the Maratta government. — A
revolution displaced him, and he threw himself under our protection. — It was natural he should make
liberal offers for our aid in re-establishing his affairs:
it was politically just that we should accept them.
Was

Was it ever imputed as a crime to the French Court
that King James was received and protected there
after his abdication? or can it be doubted that he
had bound himself to the performance of moſt am-
ple conceſſions, in caſe of a reſtoration through the
means of France? On that firſt treaty with Ragoba
you mean, I preſume, (for I have no data) to ground
the ſale of the Marattas to *him*; on the treaty of
Poorunder you muſt of courſe fix the ſale of Ragóba
to the Marattas — But here, a vote of the Houſe of
Commons authoriſes the ſale, by an approbation of
that treaty. But the ſecond and late treaty of peace
which provides a reſidence and a ſtipend in the Maratta dominions for Ragoba, nearly the ſame as was
done by the treaty of Poorunder, has another article,
by which " the Engliſh and the Peſhwa mutu-
" ally agree, that neither will afford any kind
" of aſſiſtance to the enemies of the other;" and this
inclines you to tremble for the ſafety of Ragoba. —
Had you turned to the ſixth article of the ſame
treaty, you would have ſeen that Ragoba's quiet
abode, comfortable ſupport, and perfect ſecurity,
is expreſsly provided for *by name*: and therefore if
the Peſhwa, or any of his people, offer any injury
to Ragoba as long as he continues quiet, *they*

have infringed the fixth article; and confequently the fourteenth, on which your objection is founded, will have become void of courfe.

The other Rajas and Princes whom the Company may have *fold*, are all packed up by the *dozen* or *grofs* in Woodfall's paper, fo that it is not in my power to go into the merits of each particular bargain : but from the general purport of your fpeech I am led to conclude, that let who will have been guilty of this general auction, this *fale* of Hindoftan, the Crown (or rather the prefent Miniftry) is underftood to have a right to all the benefits of a purchafer. I am not indeed yet exactly clear whether the prefent poffeffions, territories, and fovereignties belonging to the Eaft-India Company, be liable to be ranked among the *lots bought*, or the *lots fold*; but I am fure that Government exhibits at once the moft interefted eagernefs in appropriating the whole to itfelf, and the moft perfect indifference as to the validity of the title by which they are now held. To me it appears very little confonant to juftice, that the Crown fhould profit by the iniquities of the Company. Nothing can be more evident, than that the Crown was not concerned in the *acqui-*

fition

fition of the Company's prefent eftates: on what plea fhould it now affume them? If there were rapacity, or treachery, or fraud, or barbarity, in the manner by which they were firft gotten, nothing fhort of reftitution can repair the mifchief. Is it lefs rapacious, or treacherous, or barbarous, for a Government to feize the property of its own fubjects, guaranteed to them by frequent acts of its own, than for thofe fubjects to have originally feized it in the fame manner from the then lawful owners? Of the 180,000 *fquare miles*, which this Bill is to veft in the hands of . . . . I know not whom — much has been granted by public and authoritative deeds of ceffion to the Eaft-India Company: — and fuch is indifputably the tenure of the twenty-four Pergunnahs near Calcutta, and of the province of Gauzipoor and Benares. Thefe are held by grant from the Nabob of Bengal, and the Vizier of Oude, who were then fovereigns, *proprii juris,* and competent to the grant. The Dewanny of Bengal, Bahar, and Oriffa refts on a very different title, on a firmaun from the prefent Mogul, whofe power was never acknowledged in any of thofe provinces, and who by that act gave away what he never could have the

fmalleft

smallest hope of making his own. The *Dewanny* itself, considered as a Mogul establishment, confers nothing more than the appointment to collect the revenues for the Emperor's use. The internal government, the military command, are offices totally distinct, and were never, that I know or suspect, granted to the Company at all. These are branches of the *Nizamut*; and a part of them at least is still exercised under the name, and on the authority, of the Soubadar of Bengal. Surely a Bill brought into Parliament for the express display of national justice, for the declared purpose of doing away former acts of violence and oppression, a Bill which is to benefit both the Company and the Public at home, and to be the *Magna Charta* of Hindostan, should have paid some attention to these differences in the tenures of the Company's possessions. A plea of political necessity may perhaps be sufficient to wrest from them the exercise of *sovereignty*: but their *private* property should at least be inviolate. Even that despotic monarch, the Vizier of Oude, did not at once confiscate to his own use the nett collections of all the Jaghires which he took out of the hand of the Jaghiredars. There is a medium for tyranny itself to observe — and if the Company were

to

to be deprived of all power, of all credit, of all existence abroad, it would at least have been decent to have left them their houfe and warehoufes at home untouched. A whole province forcibly feized in Afia would have excited lefs murmur and indignation, than the burfting of a fingle door in Leadenhall-ftreet: and though your coufin may hector and domineer in the palace of the Rajah of Tanjore, I truft in God that the fag-ends of Mr. Fox's miniftry will have the modefty to wait a few months before they affert their fuperiority over all the dukes and peers of the realm. It cannot however be doubted, but that as foon as this bill is paffed, the very fecretary of a fecretary, the very deputies of thofe who will then be the mafters of the Crown with the title of its fervants, will have more real importance, more weight, more efficacy in the government of this devoted country, than the firft independent members of the Houfe of Lords.

Much has been faid of the infufficiency of the prefent Court of Directors to manage the Company's affairs; I believe it indeed to have been but indifferently ferved by fome few of them: and the public is at no lofs to difcover fomething more than fufpicious traces of

underhand

m......d ..e .gement. But in fact, the objections, I find, went not so much to the incapacity of the persons, as to the imperfection of their powers: and I think the four and twenty gentlemen of the present list might have been as competent to the better direction of the Company's concerns, as your sixteen new Directors, had you but given them the same enlarged authority. I would not be personal — and therefore I avoid all comparison of the present objects of preference with the rest of their brethren; as a Proprietor, however, I have something of a plea for knowledge of their several merits, and I own I am in some instances at a loss to divine the motives for their selection. You, Sir, have ascribed much of " the evils which have desolated India, to the sort " of persons sent out by the Company. Young men " without education, and with no other talents than " such as matured to rapacity and barbarity. A " *grey-beaded Englishman is a phænomenon unknown* " *in India.*" (Vide Morning Chronicle.) Mr. Hornby, surely, who has been at Bombay forty-two years, must have a wonderfully green old age, if he be not yet grey. But perhaps the *grey-beaded Receiver in the city* is not satisfied with his present pickings, and this speech is preparatory to his Indian appoint-

lies (as given away in India,) was equally unwarrantable—" A monopoly of opium" you are made to say " was fold on the moment of the contract en-" tered into for 40,000l. the next moment it was fold " for another profit ; and in the courfe of a fhort fin-" gle day, with an almoft equal enormity of advan-" tage, was fent through a variety of hands."—By this account here muft have been upwards of five lacks of rupees, perhaps ten lacks, made at once by the mere transfer of a contract from hand to hand; than which nothing was ever more remote from reafon, from probability, from fact. The whole of your information in this bufinefs arifes from the evidence of Mr. Higginfon given before your Select Committee, who mentions it as a current *report* at Calcutta that the opium contract granted to Mr. Sulivan had been by him difpofed of to another. Mr. Higginfon could not afcertain the *truth of the report* ; and I have very good grounds for believing it to be falfe. After all, the monopoly of opium, and fome other monopolies, *muft* of neceffity fubfift in fome fhape or other, as your new Directors, and new Sub-Directors, and new Governor General and Council will find—or the trade will go rapidly to ruin. I do not indeed pretend to dive into the fyftem by which the

Defpots

Defpots of the prefent bill will render their appoint-
ments a benefit to the Proprietors and the Public;
but I am fure if they tamper with the eftablifhed rou-
tine of the trade, if they unhinge the bufinefs of the
inveftment, and try *experiments* in the commercial
line, as is the fafhion in the political, the Company's
threatened infolvency will exceedingly anticipate the
clofe of their prefent commiffion.

It is curious to obferve the different grounds
on which the prefent bill has been fupported: the
Right Honourable Secretary admitted that it was a
violation of charter, but pleaded a precedent in the
act of 1773, in *that act** which you at the time fo
manfully oppofed on the very principle that it *was*
a violation. You now take the oppofite line, and
deny *this* act (which is a thoufand times more groffly
fubverfive of our rights, than the former was) to be
any violation at all—You foften it down to " the
" generous modelling of charters that had been
" ftrictly forfeited for delinquency"—You fay " the
" equity of the prefent bill is unparallelled." And
you add that " the *rights* and *property* of the
" India Company are fafe as merchants, but their
" government is juftly taken from them, as incom-
" petent

---

* See Mr. Burke's fpeeches in the Parliamentary Regifter of 1773,
printed by Almon.

" petent politicians." Facts are utterly againſt you in the whole of theſe aſſertions. The company is no longer free; its rights no longer ſubſiſt, either to the merchant, to the proprietor, or the politician. This I undertake to prove. The accurſed act of 1773 cramped them in all theſe capacities, and the preſent bill rivets their chains. It is the nature and eſſence of commerce to deal more or leſs upon credit. The merchant who ſells upon truſt, takes up money upon bills. His *real* capital ſupplies him with the means to raiſe, and authoriſes him to uſe a *fictitious* capital. He borrows money upon the ſtrength of his ſtock: and if that ſtock be clearly reſponſible, and if his trade be extenſive, his requiſitions for a loan are almoſt ſure of ſucceſs. Former acts have deprived the Company of this neceſſary reſource, of this reſource which is open to every merchant. The Company cannot borrow but of Parliament. Let its ſtock be ever ſo large, let its commerce be ever ſo flouriſhing, let its aſſets be ever ſo demonſtrably ſatisfactory, it is not permitted to avail itſelf of any or all of theſe advantages to procure an occaſional ſupply of caſh. This is the true foundation, Sir, of all the Company's calamities. The goods in the warehouſes muſt lie unſold, until the ſtated times of

fale

fale bring together the cuftomary purchafers: a glut
of the market, or any other accidental caufe, may
occafion a temporary deficiency in the amount of
the fales. But the export trade muft in the mean
time go on, the current demands muft be difcharged,
the dividends muft be regularly paid. Here *credit*
would naturally ftep in to their relief. Goods are
not *loft*, merely becaufe they are not *fold*: though a
man who does not want them, may not chufe to
purchafe them, it is not impoffible but he may lend
money at intereft upon their fecurity. Parliament
has arbitarily locked up that fecurity, has annihilated
that credit: which if it were to apply as a general
law to the tranfactions of individual merchants,
would moft affuredly bring the whole city of London to bankruptcy in fix months. Thus, then, in
this firft prohibition to borrow money, are contained
the true feeds of the Company's prefent diftreffes,
the deftruction of their rights in a mercantile capa-
city. As the influenza of *experiment* is at this
period particularly epidemic, I wifh to my foul this
abfurd prohibition were fufpended for a fhort time
by way of trial. The afflux of cafh which would
come into the Treafury, would quickly convince
you of the extent, of the ftability of the Company's

pany's credit, and fpeak more forcibly to the real profperity óf their affairs, than a thoufand unfupported affertions in a certaih Houfe can depreciate them. If this clog be deftructive of the rights of trade, there are hardfhips no lefs grievous impofed upon the proprietary. In General Courts was originally, and by charter, lodged the whole power and authority of the Company; every holder of 500l. ftock had a right to vote in this affembly, and its meetings were regulated only by expediency. Twenty-four perfons were *yearly* chofen *from among themfelves*, to manage the current bufinefs, fubject at all times to the controul of the General Court. The Proprietor of 500l. ftock has now *no* vote; *fix* Directors are now elected yearly, inftead of twenty-four, and for *four* years inftead of one. No fooner has a Director carried his election, than he flies in the face of his conftituents, holds up the act of 1773 as the bulwark of his quadrennial dictatorfhip, and perhaps negociates with the Minifter, behind the fkreen, for the erection of a new and unconftitutional tyranny on the ruin of the Company's privileges. Your *prefent* edict, which is fo *generoufly to model the charter*, will precifely effectuate this falutary purpofe. The General Court will now have

no

no controul whatfoever. It will no longer elect its
own m...nagers; *they* will be no longer chofen from
its own body; they will no longer be refponfible to
it. Even the *nine fhadows*, the make-weights of
the directorial office, will be alike indifferent to the
Proprietors' cenfure and applaufe: They are re-
movable only by their mafters, THE MIGHTY
SEVEN. The very books of accounts, fo effential
to the fatisfaction of the Proprietor, fo neceffary to
his fecurity, are no more to be open to his infpec-
tion. The report of the Company's property is to
be made by the *Commiffioners*, (I cannot bring my-
felf to call them *Directors*, till they have made their
triumphal entry into Leadenhall-ftreet) and from
that report there is no appeal. The fervile Proprietor may attend at the Quarterly General Court, like
a ftarved Parifian at the Hotel-de-Ville, gaping for
his annuity, to hear fuch a ftatement of the general
affairs, as his high and mighty Lords the *Septemviri*
fhall be gracioufly pleafed to honour him withal.
But no queftions—no whifpering—no remonftrances.
" Such, as we have laid before you, is the Com-
" pany's actual fituation; here are *our* accounts
" according to act of Parliament, and here is *your*
" dividend. Pafs your vote of thanks to my Lords
" Com-

" Commiffioners, *and dare no more approach this*
" *place, till this day three months.*" A very *generous*
model this; a very pleafant found to the ears of an
Englifhman ! But it is at beft a very accurate fketch
of the fubftance of what will be uttered *ex cathedrâ*
at the new General Courts. As the commercial and
proprietorial rights of the Company have been thus
effentially infringed by former acts of Parliament,
their political power has been no lefs cautioufly re-
ftricted. The original *Regulating Act* of 1773 en-
joined the Directors of the Eaft India Company to
communicate to his Majefty's Secretaries of State,
all the information they fhould receive refpecting the
politics of India, and all the orders they meant to
iffue in confequence. The acts of their govern-
ments, the ftate and management of their revenues,
their whole fyftem of adminiftration at large and in
detail, have been regularly fubmitted to the infpec-
tion, and (as may be prefumed from *two fingular
inflances of difapprobation* to particular paragraphs
in the Company's propofed letters to Bengal) to
the controul of his Majefty's Minifters. The Court
of Directors can neither have approved, nor cenfured
any particular meafure of their fervants *abroad*, can
neither have advifed nor prohibited any plan of policy

E   or

or any act of government *from home,* but in conformity to minifterial fentiments, but with the implied approbation of the cabinet. It fhould feem then that we
muft admit one of the two following propofitions;
Either, that his Majefty's Minifters, in not correcting
the errors, or reforming the plans of the Company's
fervants, as laid before them for examination, were
no lefs *incompetent politicians* than the Court of Directors; *or,* that adminiftration, by *purpofely* conceal-
ing its lights and with-holding its corrections, paved
the way for its own violent affumption of the power
and patronage of India, on a plea of the Company's
imbecility. If the Miniftry could fuggeft no better
mode of action than that fubmitted to them by the
prefent managers, they are alike *inadequate to the truft.*
If their opinions were ftifled, if their advice was
diffembled, and their right of approbation infidi-
oufly proftituted to ferve their own ends, they are
unworthy of it.—You have taken upon you to prove,
that the India Company have forfeited their charter,
and *therefore* that the prefent bill, which is a modi-
fication, a *modelling* of that charter, is *lenient,* is *ge-*
nerous, is *equitable, beyond parallel.* I will not afk you
how the charter has been forfeited, becaufe you will
run over your black catalogue of rapine, plunder,
robbery,

robbery, inhumanity, extortion, injuſtice, oppreſ-
ſion, and murder—upon which I ſhall not join iſſue
with you, until evidence be brought to the bar of
the Houſe. But I wiſh to know *when, at what ſpe-
cified time*, the charter was *forfeited?* If *previouſly* to
the year 1773, all your eloquence at that period was
thrown away: your abuſe of the noble Lord now in
office for his famous Regulating Act, will be deemed
to have had no more connection with *truth* than with
decency:[*] your vociferous exclamations againſt the
violation of all chartered rights in general, as included
in the violation of this one charter of the Company,
were not only daring and intemperate, but *falſe,
ſcandalous,* and *ſeditious:* your defence of the Company's ſervants of *that day,* your pamphlets, your
ſpeeches in their behalf, and in that of the great
body they ſerved, were mere convenient, catch-penny
contrivances, inſidious baits to hook in popularity.
" *Regulation*" you could then diſcover to be[†] " *injuſtice*" and " *reform*" " *robbery.*" Have words altered
their quality, has negation taken the place of aſſer-
tion, ſince that memorable æra?—I much ſuſpect it.
If you date the Company's forfeiture of their charter

* See Mr. Burke's ſpeeches in the year 1773, on the India
Regulating Act—Pubiſhed by Almon.

† Ditto.

ſubſe-

subsequently to the year 1773, for what purpose did you go back into the annals of their first establishment in Asia, and to the treaty of Illahabad? Every thing, *upon your own principles,* was right and just and legal up to that year.* " It was *necessity,* not " *choice,* that had involved the East-India Company " in war"—" They bore their own expences, *but they conquered for the state,*" (i. e. the present Ministry; and that part of your sentence has the merit of prophecy:) you cannot however deny, that the power of controul over all the politics of the Company's territories abroad has virtually rested with his Majesty's Ministers ever since 1773: so that *they* seem implicated in all the causes of forfeiture from thence up to the present day. But as a happy knack of reconciling inconsistent assertions may be one indispensable qualification to a ministerial appointment, I will admit the doctrine of necessity, in palliation of your palpable self-contradictions : wishing at the same time that they had been confined to objects of less national magnitude. In your allusion to the *Bank,* you stand, I think, alone, at least on the ministerial side of the House. Much has, no doubt, been said and felt without doors respecting the danger to which the charter of that *soul of the state* would be exposed, if the present bill should afford so glaring a precedent for its vio-

* See Mr. Burke's speeches in 1783—Published by Almon.

lation.

lation. But your happy facility of putting a queſtion is to ſilence all our murmurs, and to calm all our apprehenſions. " If the Governors, (ſays Woodfall for you) " if the clerks, or other ſervants of the Bank, had miſ- " applied the public money; if they had abuſed the " truſt repoſed in them, if they had almoſt brought " the nation to ruin, would it be unjuſt to uſe legiſ- " lative interference for the public protection ?"—No ſurely ; but then you ſhould firſt bring *evidence* of this miſapplication and breach of truſt to the bar of the Houſe : you ſhould *prove* not only that the Bank had done wrong, but that it had poſſeſſed within itſelf the means of doing right ; you ſhould *prove* that its acts had been *all its own,* and not liable to reviſion, to reformation, or ſuppreſſion, by any ſuperior authority ; you ſhould *prove* the *fact* both of the Bank's miſbehaviour, and of the injury ſuſtained by the public ; you ſhould *prove* that your legiſlative interference in behalf of the public would more than counterbalance the damage that would reſult to public credit by that very interference. Now, Sir, permit me the indulgence of a queſtion ; it ſhall be as ſhort as your's. If the rioters in 1780 had ſucceeded in their attack on the Bank ; if in ſpite of all reſiſtance made by the Directors, a mob had broken in and carried off two or three millions

in

in hard cash, would the confequent diftrefs of that body have juftified the legiflature in violating or annulling its charter ? Such is exactly the diftrefs of the Eaft-India Company, arifing principally from the loffes of trade and heavy expences incidental to the late national war. It wants nothing but a little ready money, which the legiflature will not fuffer it to raife upon *its own credit*; it is, therefore, by this cruel act, laid at the mercy of Parliament, and Parliament now ufes its power, acquired by a former ftretch of power, in *moft unmercifully* abridging the rights of the Proprietors, and new modelling (that is, annulling) the charter.———I am within bounds when I hint at the damage which will refult to public credit by this bill. Damage has *already* refulted. India ftock has fallen twenty per cent : Bank ftock (the moft folid and the moft unfluctuating of all our funds) four per cent—the three per cents above two. Is not this a clear lofs to the whole monied intereft of the nation ? a lofs, which you can never make up from the revenues of India. I repeat what I have faid in another place—that the pro uce of our territorial acquifitions in Afia can never be realized here but through the medium of the India trade. Until you can import more goods,

and

and *enfure their fale in Europe*, the country gentlemen may gape for a decreafe of the land-tax, and
the traders may petition for a recal of the ftamps,
but you will not be able to alleviate in the fmalleft
degree the burthen of either. It is demonftrable,
that the Company already import as much merchan-
dize as they can poffibly difpofe of ; and that if more
were brought to market, their price would fo exceedingly diminifh, as not only to abforb all the profits
of the trade, but even the capital. *Twenty* acts upon
the prefent plan will neither fo much benefit the Proprietors nor the public, as one which would *decifively*
and *effectually* eradicate the practice of fmuggling.
In the article of tea only, the Company is faid to
be defrauded of 1,000,000 per annum. Here is a
fubject for the difplay of patriotifm, for the exercife
of talents. Prevent this fraudulent occupation, and
you will *then* have done fomewhat towards deferving
the wonderful falaries which yourfelf and your relations enjoy from the public purfe.

You have been pleafed to confider the oppofition
which has been made to the propofed India bill, as
proceeding rather from an eager defire to overfet the
prefent Miniftry, than from a conviction of the violence

lence of the meafure. " to effect their removal,"
fay you, (I quote from Woodfall) " no means,
" however unjuftifiable, no acts, however unprece-
" dented, have been fcrupled to be practifed, or
" left untried." I moft humbly conceive, Right honourable Sir, that it is very poffible to oppofe a minifterial bill in Parliament upon principle, upon
confcience, upon conviction: that it is very decent,
perfectly *juftifiable*, and by no means *unprecedented*,
to prefent an *account* at the bar, when a matter of
account is to be argued: and that thofe perfons who
think their fortunes or privileges endangered by the
operation of a new bill, are at liberty to publifh
their thoughts upon the fubject, pending the difcuffion of the bill in either houfe. *Unjuftifiable means*,
and *unprecedented acts*, I take to be fuch as the *following*; an infidious advertifement promifing 1000
guineas for a writer's place at Bengal — The offer
of 100l. for difcovery of the writer of an incendiary
letter, which moft affuredly was never written —
The induftrious circulation of idle and groundlefs
ftories of the Governor General's death, of his being
crowned king of Bengal, or of his having involved
the nation in a new war — An exclufion of impartial (or if you will, anti-minifterial) difcuffions on

fubjcts

fubjects of national importance, from the daily pa-
pers, by money. — By whom, and for what purpofe,
fuch acts have been applied (and the facts alluded
to are of the moft open and barefaced notoriety) it
becomes not me to conjecture; but I will whifper in
your ear, that they do not come from the oppofers of
the bill.

As it is perfectly underftood, Sir, by the public,
that in the prefent addrefs I am not guilty of an un-
neceffary, voluntary, or officious prefumption, that
I now write merely in conformity to the known functions of my miffion, and *from no perfonal motive
whatever*, I cannot lay down my pen without advert-
ing to a few circumftances, which, though not imme-
diately contained in the *fpeech* I have juft done my-
felf the honour to difcufs, are yet intimately con-
nected with the fubject before us, are of the ut-
moft confequence to my *Principal*, and are generally
allowed to *proceed from you*. A moment's reflection
will inform you that I allude to the *eleventh Report
from the Select Committee*. So criminatory a performance, fo artfully interwoven with hints of myfteri-
ous concealment, with infinuations of guarded cor-
ruption, with mutilated extracts, and partial deduc-

F . tions,

tions, has not, I believe, been frequently expofed to public notice. It is not without concern, Sir, that I have perufed this fingular production, becaufe, as you pointedly ftate in the work itfelf, *" Mr. Scott " profeffed himfelf perfectly uninftructed upon almoft " every part of the fubject."* I now again affure you in the moft folemn manner, that I have never received the fmalleft inftruction upon the tranfactions alluded to in your Eleventh Report, and that this total filence of Mr. Haftings to me on the feveral articles *there* exhibited, conveys to my mind an irrefiftible conviction of his perfect innocence. As you have obligingly *recorded my incapacity* to defend my Principal on points where he never expected an attack, it would have been worthy of Mr. Burke's *known humanity* to have furnifhed the public with at leaft all thofe flender documents that *do fubfift*, to have generoufly affifted my incapacity by the communication of thofe lights which enabled *him* to fee his way fo clearly through the mift of the prefent bufinefs, *to have publifhed the Appendix together with the Report.* At fuch a critical moment to with-hold fo confiderable and fo neceffary a part of the evidence, *for twelve days already*, and I know not how much longer the delay may endure, would in any

other

other man have been deemed cruel, indelicate, and unfair. Of circumstances so insidiously arranged, so partially worked up, and so imperfectly displayed, men can hardly have the chance of forming a liberal, candid, and favourable opinion: that they are mysterious at best, that they are so unfortunately obscure, as to be incapable of satisfactory explanation in their present state, I readily acknowledge, and I have already acknowledged it to your Committee; but it is now incumbent on me to announce, *what in justice you ought to have announced in the Report*, that Mr. Hastings has informed the Court of Directors of his readiness to answer all questions respecting his receipt and disposal of presents " *upon his l
our and upon his oath.*" It will be too late to read this six months hence in your Appendix; your turn will have been long served, and the prejudice you intended to raise will have had full time to operate. But such concerns of the Governor General as relate to money, are out of my department; I can only declare upon my conscience and before God, that I know his fortune in England to be quite incompetent to his rank in life, that I never knew him to have expended a shilling in the purchase of any corrupt influence either

ther

ther here or abroad — that no grounds have ever been traced on which to found a plaufible fufpicion of any fuch tranfaction, and that I will ftake my life upon his integrity.

I fhall now, Sir, take my leave, with profound acknowledgements for the very polite and liberal manner in which you were pleafed *yefterday* to turn me out of that moft humane, impartial, juft, and free affembly, *the Select Committee.* My intrufion proceeded from the miftaken notion that *Your's was an open Committee.*

I am, with all refpect,

Right Honourable Sir,

\ Your moft obedient,

Humble Servant,

J O H N S C O T T.

LONDON,
December 6, 1783.